Dream interiors

Dream interiors

Author

Francisco Asensio Cerver

Editorial

manager

Paco Asensio

Design

and layout

VERSUS

Text

Richard Rees

Elaine Fradley

Proofreading

Elaine Fradley

Photographers

Eugèni Pons
Jordi Miralles
Imanol Sistiaga
Chris Gascoigne

© Copyright 1998 Francisco Asensio Cerver

Published by:

arco editorial, s.a.

Ganduxer 115, 4º
Barcelona 08022 Spain.
T. 34-3-418 49 10
Fax 34-3-211 81 39
email:arcoedit@idgrup.ibernet.com

ISBN: 84-8185-176-0

Printed in Spain

Glosary

Intro

Decoration forms part of life. Thanks to it our homes are transformed into genuine mirrors of our personality, reflecting habits and manias, interests and tastes. It finds nourishment in our memories and experiences and grows and develops with us, adapting to the passage of time and to new needs.

duction

When we observe an interior, it tells us something about its owner, allowing us to guess the nature of his/her moods and spirit. Some rooms speak to us of quiet, family-loving individuals; others of practical, dynamic people, lovers of social and urban life; and still others, naturally, of sensitive, romantic characters who love to daydream. For this reason it is vitally important that the decor chosen should be faithful to ourselves, to our expectations and dreams, and to our personal way of looking at the world.

This book is meant to be a model and source of inspiration for all those who want to decorate their house. It provides ideas and suggests a number of interesting decorative resources. It presents all present-day trends in interior decorating all over the world, from the most traditional to the most innovative, and offers the reader a selection of interiors that, for one reason or another and regardless of style, are truly captivating.

The next few pages briefly describe the different themes to be found in the book.

Layout

All the interiors featured here are arranged according to a logic in which empty spaces and volumes alternate in perfect harmony, different environments are suitably delimited, and free, unobstructed movement is guaranteed. The photographs show on the one hand original, exuberant spaces crammed with an overwhelming abundance of decorative elements. By contrast, other interiors leave considerable amounts of space free thanks to a frugal, restrained use of decorative elements. And carrying this to an extreme, still other interiors are genuinely minimalist, in which the decor is restricted to indispensable elements so that the rooms themselves come close to the absolute void.

Materials

Different building materials each define their own spaces and endow them with a particular character. Thus, natural stone reigns supreme in rustic interiors; as do terra cotta, solid wood and wrought iron. More modern interiors are dominated by pale wood, concrete, plant fiber, lacquers, ceramics and parquet. For their part, avant-garde urban interiors favor steel, acid-treated glass and bare brick.

Colors

We cover the whole color spectrum by showing interiors for all tastes and moods: pure, innocent rooms in immaculate, ethereal, almost celestial white that invite meditation; serene spaces whose colors are chosen from a limited palette of kindred tones; explosions of color in which contrast is the absolute protagonist and in which the most vivid reds stand opposite electric blues, tempestuous tones and astonishing prints.

Decorative Styles

We present a wide range of decorative styles, since nowadays anything goes. We offer very modern interiors, easy to understand and rapidly accepted; rustic houses of a timeless, country-style beauty; romantic decors, soft and almost feminine, and hard, metallic, industrial, masculine environments; urban corners for uncompromising city-lovers; youthful, refreshing Mediterranean marine environments; interiors in period style; avant-garde rooms and respectful art nouveau restorations.

Balance and Rhythm

Rhythm and balance are two highly important decorative factors, since they are largely responsible for the overall verdict on the end result.

Balance can be achieved in many ways: by suitably arranging the seating; by placing ornamental objects in one way or another; by seeking perfect symmetry or deliberately breaking it. The repetition of certain resources guarantees rhythm that, occasionally and in order to add dynamism, may be brusquely interrupted.

Luxury and Austerity

On occasion, decors may be simple and restrained, discreet and modest, shunning excess and ostentation, relaxing styles at odds with overwhelming luxury. In these cases natural elements are used, extracted from the earth, which remind us of our origins and speak to us of Nature. Austerity is the most sought-after quality and frankness the most prized virtue.

There are times, however, when just the opposite occurs, when wealth is openly displayed. Then we find an abundance of sophisticated furniture, large paintings, pieces of incalculable value. Roman busts, classical sculptures, walls decorated with highly elaborate frescoes, gilt details, striking borders and so on. A highly personal universe in which nothing is superfluous.

Textiles

Practical, youthful, fresh textiles predominate. Blinds are preferred to classic curtains, and plain carpets, check upholstery, whites, ochers and creams are in vogue.

Carpets, cushions and bedspreads are occasionally called upon to provide touches of color in otherwise monochrome environments. And in rustic and period environments there is a predominance of delicate, semi-transparent lace curtains, white linen and lace.

Lighting

Most of the photographs show interiors that open onto the exterior through huge glazed doors, many of which are of the sliding type. Light floods in, all-pervading and potentiating the beauty of colors and textures. Sometimes it is more tempered by curtains or blinds or else it filters mischievously through windows and cracks, allowing furtive beams to spatter the objects they touch with their magical glow. There is an abundance of interplays between light and shadow, mysterious and evocative, which conceal and transform reality, endowing it with new meanings.

Artificial light enters the scene when natural light disappears, in the form either of concentrated spots or small, strategically placed lamps.

Furniture

Classic, rustic, modern, avant-garde: there is furniture for all tastes; although the dominant trend is a mixture of styles. In this way, antique desks, Elizabethan chests of drawers and Chester-type easy chairs take their place naturally beside elegant trunks on castors, multicolored easy chairs or plant-fiber accessories.

There is also an abundance of modular or made-to-measure furniture, pieces that adapt masterfully to the characteristics and irregularities of the spaces that house them. Self-mounting metallic industrial structures are the latest fashion, while spacious sofas with large cushions are the protagonists of seating arrangements.

Decorative Accessories

Although these are not always given their due importance, their presence helps to achieve a certain rhythm, to establish an ambience or define the owners' personality. Pictures greatly beautify interiors and, depending on how they are hung, different decorative effects are obtained. When arranged geometrically they provide order and classicism, marking a steady, traditional rhythm; if they are arranged to form asymmetrical or irregular groups they create an impression of deliberate chaos, highly appropriate for youthful, informal rooms.

Plants provide freshness and vitality, since they are the only living elements that form part of a decor. Sometimes they are used to hide awkward corners or to establish balance. Cushions, pitchers, statuettes, in short mementoes of experiences and special moments, tend to be used as visual counterpoints or else as striking notes of color to break monotony.

Living rooms and Dining rooms

This book presents living rooms and dining rooms in all styles and for all tastes. Classic, rustic, postmodern, up-to-date and youthful, casual and practical decors; white, luminous, traditional, urban spaces, suitable for country or beach houses. A great number of dining, coffee and occasional tables appear; a wide variety of easy chairs and sofas, although white pieces abound; chests of drawers, crockery cabinets, console tables, fireplaces: elements all capable of creating unique environments.

Kitchens

A wide range of possibilities: classic white-tiled kitchens with rustic furniture; industrial-style kitchens, cold and metallic; cheerful, colorful kitchens, characterised by an almost naif charm; kitchens with pantry, either independent or joined to the living-dining room.

Bedrooms

The decorative value of bathrooms increases daily. They demand considerable dedication and are usually considered as a status symbol. The key material is glazed mosaic tiling, usually blue, and the piece to which most attention is devoted the bathtub. The most common washbasins are of steel with the plumbing in full view, or double white basins built into elegant wooden tops. They require correct installation of artificial lighting.

Bathrooms

These are the most private, personal rooms in the whole house, and many provide the key to an understanding of its decor: romantic, rustic, minimalist, cluttered, youthful bedrooms whose aesthetics might be similar to or completely different from that of the rest of the house. Sometimes they are integrated into the overall decor and separated from the more social areas by a light structure; on other occasions they are more retiring and retreat behind conventional walls and doors.

Decoration is an art, a complex art difficult to define. We might stringently follow its rules and establish perfect, harmonious balances; we might arrange the different decorative elements with calculated symmetry and choose furniture of beautiful design and high quality. We might paint the walls in fashionable colors and cover the floor with the best materials. And yet, having done this, we might realise that something has gone wrong, things have not turned out as we planned. Something is missing: life.

When we decorate our home we have to look around us and compare styles and trends, but this is not enough. We must also be faithful to our own personality and put something of ourselves into each room. Only in this way will we manage to create a house with soul.

Present and past

These two bedrooms are radical opposites: one is classically rustic and could well have belonged to our grandparents. The other, by contrast, is youthful and very natural. Both, in their own way, are equally charming and charged with distinction.

The nostalgic bedroom reflects the beauty of farmhouse interiors, with its bare wooden beams, the sturdy doors, and the old sewing machine transformed into a console table. Elements that further enhance this effect are the sober, austere bedside tables, and above all the exquisitely romantic wrought-iron bed with its linen sheets.

One's impressions change on observing the second bedroom, though they remain equally positive. The ambience continues to be romantic, although the archaic characteristics that define the previous example are absent here. The rustic wrought-iron bed has been replaced by a more schematic model beneath an elegant canopy. The antiques have been eliminat-

ed in favor of avant-garde furniture. The walls are electric blue, the sharp coldness of this tone being offset by the use of wood. As in the previous case, the ceiling beams have been left bare.

As the beauty of these two examples shows, successful decors are not a question of style. Each of the two interiors possesses its own charm, its character, its "raison d'être". We must observe them with an open mind and choose the one that best suits our personality.

These two bedrooms show us different ways of evoking a single image. While the first is a literal reproduction of the decor and ambience of an old-fashioned bedroom, the second brings an abstraction and simplification of detail to point up a present-day reworking of the theme.

The wrought-iron bed is the main protagonist of this decor.

The color blue endows this bedroom with character.

Welcoming surroundings

Fresh and luminous, the ambiences of this dwelling base their beauty on simplicity; and it may be for this reason that the atmosphere created transmits a special feeling of serenity, able to ease even the most troubled mind.

The interior seems to be a prolongation of the exterior, since both share the common denominator of terracotta flooring. The large windows provide views of the garden, which can be enjoyed without leaving the house, while the unobstructed light freely enters through the different corners, enveloping everything in its particular embrace.

The key piece is the living-dining room, in which all family activity takes place. The living area is dominated by a modern fireplace with its canopy and draft in full view. The center table is simple in design, with firm, straight lines, and the seating consists of two garnet-colored sofas. A sisal rug lies on the floor, particularly suitable for second-home type dwellings such as this.

For its part, the dining room is furnished with an elegant, light rectangular table with an acid-treated glass top and highly stylized legs, and a set of very up-to-date chairs. Behind the dining-room table a cantilevered stair leads to the floor above.

The living room is dominated by a modern fireplace.

The interior seems to be the prolongation of the exterior.

The bedroom echoes the simple, youthful style of the living-dining room. The walls are painted pale yellow, a relaxing color that creates the impression of spaciousness.

This interior is a good example of how good taste is often based on simplicity and restraint.

The recourse to simple finish in elements like the fireplace and the stair produces an almost sculptural effect, like works on show in the clear white halls of an art gallery.

The staircase in particular is suggestive of a great backbone. Each step recalls a vertebra in a metaphor which points up the importance of this architectural element to the life of the house.

A similar situation is produced by the choice of certain old pieces of furniture. The small trunk pressed into service as a bedside table takes on major protagonism in the absence of other furniture and decorative elements.

Each element comes into its own in relation to its immediate context. Many of the best organized spaces in this house revolve around contrast. The most significant elements are carefully isolated; what better way to point up a scene than placing it in an irrelevant setting?

Simplicity is the main characteristic of this interior decor.

A clean, relaxing atmosphere has been created for the bedroom.

An amalgam of elements

Nobody could possibly remain indifferent to this interior: the eyes of the astonished visitor will scrutinize every corner, discovering pieces of curious provenance and little-used resources.

The mixture of elements and styles is the key to this kind of decor, in which anything apparently goes. Thus smooth white walls offset the deliberate crudeness of highly original frescoes. At the same time, several partial partitions break what would otherwise be monotonous symmetry. On the ceiling the wooden beams add a touch of tradition to this eclectic interior, while the flooring is used to separate spaces by assigning a different type (parquet and mosaic) to each individual environment.

This interior consists of two rectangular rooms. The larger of the two is a living room in which the latest designs combine with exotic or ethnic furniture. Next to the

In the background, an original living room. In the foreground, a curious piece of design furniture.

This photograph shows the curious mixture of motley elements that characterizes this interior.

living room, the library, characterized by an abundance of light modular elements. The other room acts as a study, in which the furniture chosen reinterprets the style typical of offices. The elegant presence of a grand piano is a factor of both disorientation and seduction.

One of the greatest merits of this room is the correct though highly unusual subdivision into environments. The separating elements themselves perform an essential decorative function. This is the case of the flooring or the partitions.

The idea here is not to define a perfect, finished space with a place for everything and everything in its place, but to furnish an ambience where the rooms enjoy a degree of freedom, with layouts which are the result of daily routines rather than military precision.

In this way, the old and the new come together in almost random fashion, obeying neither hierarchies nor rules. A crumbling wall or worn beam become as important to the house as a specially designed piece of furniture.

The first concern of rehabilitation is to respect the given circumstances. A space does not need to be rebuilt to bring it up to date (in many cases this would be its death knell); it needs to be looked at with new eyes and reassessed.

The piano: a romantic element tempers the cold atmosphere of the study.

The study is a reinterpretation of the office style.

Open spaces

A wooden partition, with a sliding door, separates the living room from the study.

This is an interior of open, interrelated spaces in which the original, avant-garde structure of the dwelling seems to assume the leading role. The furniture is minimal —only those pieces have been used whose absence would make living in the house uncomfortable—, though sufficient, and the environments created astonish by virtue of their serenity and studied minimalism.

In the living room the attention is attracted by a spectacular bare brick vaulted ceiling. In order not to eclipse the beauty of this architectural resource, the chosen furniture is simple and discreetly toned. Only an easy chair and a pouffe, both in bright red, break the color monotony.

The structural divisions are apparently flexible, almost provisional. Thus a wooden partition separates the living room from the room next door —a well-lit study—, and a wide sliding door provides access from one to the other.

The study decor is limited to a rectangular wooden desk on sturdy metal trestles. The chairs and the bookshelf hanging from the wall add to the reigning aesthetic futurism.

Finally, the bedroom is characterized above all by its visual hygiene, achieved thanks to a wise combination of tones.

Decorating a home of large dimensions with only a few elements and leaving many spaces open is a risky option. Generally speaking, though, the results are satisfactory; indeed, in this case they are unsurpassable.

The furniture of the living room enhances the beauty of the architectural structure.

Reserved corners

Not so long ago the bathroom was considered a private, discreetly concealed area. Today, however, it tends to be openly exhibited, money is lavished on it and it is often taken to be a sign of the owners' financial status.

In one of the interiors presented on these pages, the bathroom has ceased to be a taboo to the extent that it forms an active part of the bedroom decor. A partial partition, open on one side, endows the area containing the bath and the toilet with privacy. The sanitary ware, on the other hand, is concealed behind a door painted bright blue.

The second bathroom is adapted in dimensions and format to the peculiarities of the sloping roof of an attic. One of the walls is occupied by a made-to-measure cupboard with numerous drawers and containers that fits like a glove into the available space.

The sanitary ware and bath are in white, as is the washbasin top, a color most suitable for this kind of element by virtue of the visual cleanliness it transmits. There is a danger, however, that the chosen elements become excessively cold and aseptic. In this case, the use of wood guarantees the necessary warmth.

The bathrooms presented in this article are highly personal and welcoming. Their elements are perfectly well distributed and designed according to the rules of common sense.

The cupboard and the cladding have had to adapt to the slope of the ceiling.

This bathroom forms part of the bedroom decor.

Warm wood

Wood envelops every corner of this house, endowing them with unity and a nobility that only this material, the quintessence of warmth, is able to provide.

Outstanding among the elements that form the inner structure is the stair, which acts as a distributor and organizer of space. On the ground floor, it separates a small living room from a half-empty area used as an improvized art gallery. The living area is furnished with a springy white sofa accompanied by two armchairs of the same characteristics. Among these pieces there is a stylized auxiliary table and on the floor an attractive set of oriental rugs. In the exhibition space, there is a beautiful contrast between the wood and the sky-blue back wall.

The stair leads to the floor above, where the doors are totally integrated into the wooden structure to the point where they become almost invisible.

The stair serves as an element to separate different environments.

The living room is decorated with cheerful furniture.

But perhaps the most successful environment is the bathroom, characterized by modern, innovative design. Wood continues to cover walls and ceiling, interrupted only by the ceramics of the washbasin and toilet and the mirror. A central column breaks the space, creating different visual planes. And to prevent an excess of wood from making the room too dark, the ceiling features a huge skylight, thanks to which the bathroom is a veritable explosion of luminosity among suggestive chiaroscuros.

Wood warmly embraces each of the corners of this dwelling, although its sober tones might have robbed the different environments of freshness. To prevent the wood interiors from becoming oppressive, it is necessary to offset its dominant visual presence with light, youthful furniture, which is precisely what the designers of this interior have done.

The doors are entirely integrated into the wooden structure.

Wood also features in the bathroom.

Attention to detail

The aim of this article is to present a series of details which often go unnoticed because they are not included in the main rooms of the house, though they are just as important –if not more so– for the smooth running of the home.

The photographs show us bathroom doors and shelving systems in corridors. It is unlikely that anyone should look back at this kind of space as being the most remarkable feature after a visit to a house; yet the proper arrangement of fittings is more important here than in the most spacious rooms, because they are almost always small spaces into which a variety of furnishings, fixtures and electrical appliances have to be fitted.

The photographs on these pages show us tremendously subtle details, like this bathroom door, covered with glazed mosaic, as though it were part of the wall. If we don't know where the door is, we could almost walk past it without noticing. However, the marble flooring passes through the door to announce the presence of the bathroom in less evident fashion. The wooden shelves are surrounded by glass. The transparent strips above and below the furniture allow us to see the space in its entirety, at the same time ensuring visual independence between the passage and the rooms.

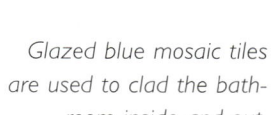

Glazed blue mosaic tiles are used to clad the bathroom inside and out.

A Temple of peace

The bathroom that illustrates these pages has been decorated as a room devoted to the care of the body and health. Its generous dimensions provide plenty of room for maneuver and its great visual cleanliness fosters relaxation.

The gresite cladding provides unity.

The walls are entirely clad in stone-colored gresite, though spattered with tiny sky-blue mosaics to discreetly break the chromatic monotony. For its part, the paving adds its own color (also sky blue) to the touches that give life to the walls. The furniture is modern, without being either nostalgic or avant-garde. The pale wood of the fittings, identical to that of the stylized door, endows the room with a certain youthful freshness. The polished marble surface features two washbasins, while a mirror occupying the whole wall visually duplicates the space.

At the opposite end of the bathroom stands the piece that endows it with distinction and character: a large, round bath that enjoys all the light entering through a big window that fits perfectly into the wall. The bath is embedded into a raised platform clad in glazed mosaic, and access to it is by means of two wide steps. On one of the sides of the structure, a glazed partition separates it from the shower.

Thanks to the use of few elements with mosaic as the unifying factor, this bathroom is both hygienic and comfortable and invites the user to relax.

The bath is the star attraction.

Urban landscapes

The rooms that feature on the following pages are very different in that they share neither styles, nor color, nor decor solutions. Even so, there is something that unites them: all three would be perfectly suitable for urban residences since they abound in straight lines, metallic elements and gray tones.

One of them is an aseptic-looking kitchen. Natural light enters through a long, narrow frameless window while artificial light is provided by a number of recessed lights strategically placed in the ceiling. The kitchen appliances and furniture are placed beneath a white top that unifies them.

The second room is part of a former warehouse that has been refurbished as a home. In this room, which acts as a kitchen-dining room, the high vaulted ceiling hides the spotlights while providing depth. The cupboards are part wooden, part metallic, light and adaptable, while the dining-room table consists of a sheet of glass resting on a steel structure.

Finally, the bathroom features the straight line, which substitutes the rounded forms normally found in this kind of room. Thanks to the wall mirror, with a number of recessed lights above, the room seems to double its size.

Urban ambiences should recreate, as these do, aspects of city reality. The resulting image is at once modern and masculine.

Although the lounge is not a large one, both the table and sofa areas seem spacious and comfortable, an effect which required cutting back the amount of furniture to the strictly necessary. In this way, the living room fulfill its functions perfectly without overcrowding.

Straight lines replace the traditional rounded forms of bathrooms.

The kitchen is characterized by straight lines and the total absence of decorative elements.

Wood, metal and glass: three highly modern materials with which to decorate an old warehouse.

Dazzling white

White irradiates light; it is the color of innocence and hope-filled joy. It elevates the senses and defines ambiences of calm elegance unaffected by the passage of time, since they remain on the fringe of the dictates of whimsical fashion.

In these two rooms, white is used as the basic argument. Both enjoy considerable luminosity, potentiated by the whiteness of walls and furniture, although the decorative resources employed in each case are different. The parquet floor of one of the rooms plays down the visual impact of the shining white. The structure of the room is irregular and appears to be delimited by the dwelling's facade, which features a number of impressive arched windows. A sofa for three, a chaise longue and an armchair occupy most of the space. The traditional bookshelf has been replaced by a light, hanging model.

In the second room, white predominates even more: only the carpets and the iron fireplace break the overall uniformity. The false ceiling that conceals a number of spotlights is one of the room's main attractions: it seems to be the continuation of the side blinds and provides clear, transparent light. The decor is completed with a large modern sofa, another in the chesterfield style and two or three psychedelic chairs.

The two rooms are characterized by their magic, diaphanous, almost otherworldly atmosphere. In a way they evoke the past. They are conducive to inner peace.

The false ceiling is one of the main attractions of this room.

The parquet offsets the predominant white.

Highly personal

In order for a bedroom to reflect the personality of its owners, only a few details are needed: the color of the walls, the texture of the different cloths, the design of the furniture. Each tiny element has its part to play in the creation, defining a style and establishing specific decorative criteria.

Discreet and relaxing, this bedroom combines different pastel shades of blue with brilliant white. The mixture is so cleverly made that all the colors seem to meld into each other, giving rise to wonderful new nuances.

All that can be seen of the bed is the head —two large squares of wood—, and one of its metal legs. This piece is covered by practical, elegant linen, sober and urbane. The bedspread in particular is the most vivid note of color in the room and its presence contributes a great deal to the avoidance of much-feared aesthetic monotony. The tables on either side of the bed match the head, while the white easy chair with wood finishes elegantly balances the decor. Other outstanding elements are the clothes basket and the picture on the wall.

This interior's main virtue is the masterful arrangement of furniture and ornamental objects, which together constitute an incomparable example of balance. The different elements adapt to a garret-like space, creating an ambience that faithfully reflects the owners' serene character.

This interior is a fine example of aesthetic balance.

The wooden bedhead is one of the most attractive pieces in the room.

Living spaces

The spaces inside this dwelling are neither immutable nor rigid. On the contrary, the interior reality of the house creates the impression of movement and variability, of restless dynamism.

More or less dense volumes interrupt each other, creating new spaces that while perfectly well defined are at once linked and separated. Taking the study-library as an example, and observing the room in all its depth, we see different visual planes superimposed on one another. The tall wall-to-wall bookshelf is joined to a vaulted bridge that creates a new ambience. In the background, higher up, we glimpse a new room with its own bookshelf. A large, sloping-top work desk stands on a plant fiber rug.

One of the bedrooms is minimalist in design, all its surface being almost completely bare. Wood covers both floors and walls, with the single exception of one wall in bare brick. On the floor, a comfortable futon rests on a tatami.

Another of the rooms is vaguely oriental in style, with its abundance of rugs, twisted lamps and a wicker chair, whose sinuous forms recall those of a cobra.

Given the marked architectural character of the house, the decor takes second place, being required to elegantly offset these intelligent structures without either concealing or masking them.

One of the bedrooms is minimalist in style.

Gentle exoticism impregnates the corners of another bedroom.

The bookshelf is linked to a vaulted bridge that creates a new space.

The mediterranean spirit

All the light of Mediterranean landscapes seems to form part of this unusually fresh and imposing bedroom. The white recalls surf; the pale-colored wood of the furniture echoes the warmth of sand that stretches along endless beaches; and the bright blue of a number of small details is the living expression of waters imbued with history.

The white marble surface of the floor becomes rough wood when we cross the threshold to the terrace. The transition is so gentle, however, that interior and exterior seem to form part of the same ambience. The large, sliding, wall-to-wall glass doors temper the occasionally excessive light with two roller blinds, white like the rest and plasticized as protection against salt spray. Romantic curtains prevent these possibly too prosaic, functional blinds from spoiling an otherwise beautiful, almost ethereal ambience.

The bed, though schematic and simple, is a robust piece of furniture with a soft, inviting mattress and two twin pillows. A sideboard with numerous drawers completes the furnishing. A colonial-style fan hangs from the ceiling and the classical bedside tables have been replaced by curious rectangular niches containing shelves. On the wall, an abstract painting provides a touch of bright color.

Coastal interiors, like this one, should always allow light to be the protagonist, blatantly flooding and taking possession of the different ambiences.

The transition between interior and exterior is astonishingly smooth.

The abstract painting on the wall stands out against an otherwise white setting.

A summer house

With its ceramic flooring, cool upholstery and total lack of carpeting, this living-dining room seems to have been designed specially for the summer months. Its corners are of a clean, relaxing beauty and are characterized by a certain economy of elements and discreet colors.

Large glass doors occupy two of the walls, through which natural light pours and bounces off the white surfaces that abound in the room. The living area is of moving simplicity, the furniture consisting of a large sofa, three easy chairs and a pouffe, all in white. In the middle, a transparent table stands on sturdy legs. Behind the sofa there is a bookcase in wood and glass.

The dining room, like the living room, shuns decorative excess and vivid colors. The sober, right-angled table is surrounded by schematic chairs with bluish Alcántara upholstery, an aesthetic typical of modern offices. At the far end, leaning against the wall, a chest of drawers divided into several compartments presides over the room.

Thanks to the design project, this room shines with its own light: the astonishing harmony of its environments, based on simplicity, combines with clever touches of color that prevent the all-pervading coolness from becoming ice-cold.

Although the lounge is not a large one, both the table and sofa areas seem spacious and comfortable, an effect which required cutting back the amount of furniture to the strictly necessary. In this way, the living room fulfill its functions perfectly without overcrowding.

The dining room: aesthetic simplicity with markedly urban touches.

Light floods into the room through the glass doors.

From the hill

The colors on the walls create different visual planes.

This house enjoys a privileged position on top of a hill with the city at its feet. Decorative elements have been reduced to a minimum, passing the leading aesthetic role to the high-quality architectural structure.

One of the environments featured on these pages is the living room, which opens onto a terrace barely defined by a kerb. The ceiling and the large door providing access to the terrace consist of a framework of wooden slats and glazed surfaces that creates an interplay of light and shadow which captivates the sensitive observer. A yellow sofa for three, a bench in the same color and a wooden center table are the only pieces of furniture. Other, superfluous elements might have concealed the beauty of such an exceptional architectural environment.

In the bedroom the colors create different visual planes that are both surprising and pleasing. Three walls are white and luminous, like the wardrobes that adapt to the profile of the columns at the entry, the counterpane and the ceiling. The fourth wall has been painted in an unusual color, bitter orange, and the effect obtained could not be better: besides breaking the chromatic unity, it acts as the center of interest and adds depth to the room.

The environments decorated with the minimum number of pieces of furniture leave a considerable amount of space free, while their elegance enhances the constructional quality of the dwelling. On the other hand, it is not always easy to do without furniture and ornamental objects.

The living room opens onto a large terrace without handrails.

A rustic flavor

A series of unusual details arranged on an ocher or red background turn this house into a constant succession of surprises: the eye-catching bed head, with its canopy hanging down to either side; the little round tables in the living room, which could have been taken from a magic show; and particularly the fireplace, clad with blue mosaic and partly painted with vertical blue and orange stripes, a detail which is picked up by the sofa upholstery.

The bathroom is worthy of particular attention. Rather larger in size than these spaces tend to be, with the privilege of having a window to let daylight in, this room ceases to be a utilitarian space for a hurried wash before rushing off to work and become an invitation to relax and enjoy.

The surface surrounding the wash basins and the little wall around the bath tub are built with bricks which were then clad with a reddish stucco similar to the tone used in the bedroom. A large wall-to-wall mirror runs above the wash basins for greater ease of use and to visually duplicate the space. The mirror is bordered by a strip of blue mosaic, which is also used to clad the side of the bath. The bathroom is decorated with friezes, patterns and other details in blue on the walls, tiles and fittings.

Views of the living room and bathroom.

Detail of the master bedroom.

Power to the imagination

The decor of this curious room breaks molds and improvises with daring, introduces vivid colors with restraint and creates spaces at once useful and tremendously original.

The room, brightly lit thanks to the glazed terrace doors, is arranged as a living room and library. To allow for unencumbered circulation, the different elements are accumulated on the periphery, leaving the center empty and free, thus clearing what would otherwise appear to be a very cramped room. An overall glance at the room reveals that what is most outstanding is the masterful use of color, since subdued tones are combined with vivid ones, disguising defects and potentiating virtues. Thus, for example, the marble flooring, somewhat wan in appearance, seems to be revived thanks to the colorful vitality of the sofas and oriental rugs.

At one end of the room a metal spiral stair leads down to the floors below. The area enclosed by this structure, delimited by a large wooden cupboard and frames in the same material, has been painted a pale yellow, tempered here and there by orange tones. And located between the stair and the wall is the library, perfectly adapted to the characteristics of this small corner.

If it were not for the use of daring colors and original structures, this interior might have sunk into urban monotony, and resulted insipid and conventional. Nonetheless, and to offset this, it was decided to adopt a daring, personal and innovative decor.

The sofa, one of the main notes of color.

A small library stands next to the stair.

Reflections in glass

The platform on which the bed stands is transformed into a large study desk.

The interiors that comprise this home, specifically a dining room and youthful bedroom, are spaces of original elegance thanks to interesting decorative solutions.

The corridor is integrated into the dining room, and on one of the walls a number of column-like vertical modules have been placed, joined together by three shelves. The wood that envelops the room, covering walls, ceiling and floor, unifies environments and provides personality and warmth. On the other hand, one of the dining room walls has been replaced by a translucent glass partition that, besides providing a touch of pleasant modernity, projects beautiful reflections onto the polished surfaces. The table is a stylized, almost schematic rectangular model accompanied by a quartet of chairs with arms and Alcántara upholstery.

In the bedroom, the most intelligent solution is the prolongation of the platform on which the bed stands, converting it into a large, comfortable study desk. This is possible thanks to the fact that the room is structured on two different levels. Wood also abounds in the bedroom, although not to the same extent as in the dining room.

Originality is not something exclusive to avant-garde environments. As this dwelling shows, it is possible to be innovative without being too audacious.

The corridor is integrated into the dining room, and both areas are completely clad in wood.

Making full use of the space

Today it is extremely difficult, not to say impossible, to find a large home. In most cases people have to be content with apartments of modest dimensions, in which to fit furniture and all kinds of personal objects without causing absolute disorder.

The first thing that strikes the visitor to this pleasant home is the fact that the different environments breathe, despite having been exploited almost millimeter by millimeter. The secret of this success lies in the removal of all rigid barriers and the subsequent creation of interrelated rooms that share spaces and colors. The corridor acts as distributor, leading to a totally open-plan kitchen with a different floor covering.

The rooms are closed by partial partitions which also act as cupboards or practical containers. In the case of one of the bedrooms, the partition becomes a bookcase on its inner side. The high ceiling in this room has made it possible to build a small mezzanine half-floor.

Color performs an important function in this interior: that of differentiating between environments. White walls stand opposite yellow ones, interrupted by the ultramarine partitions. Parquet gives way to dark ceramic flooring in the kitchen.

Not everyone has sufficient talent to take advantage of minimum space. In this case, however, the environments have been created with great skill, obtaining square footage where there seemed to be none.

The kitchen is totally open-plan.

A long bookshelf has been built in the corridor that leads into the different rooms.

Overlooking the sea

Beside the mighty, proud sea stands this refreshing, youthful and colorist home, characterized by an abundance of well-exploited corners and the exemplary use of decorative resources.

The interior echoes the placid beauty of the house exterior; consequently, the rooms impress the visitor by virtue of their atmosphere of welcoming hospitality. They are radiant, genial, luminous and tremendously vital. In consonance with modern architecture, the different spaces are united and interrelated. Each corner is therefore a genuine Pandora's box of surprises, concealing a marvelous new environment.

False wooden partitions interrupt walls whose brickwork is lightly disguised beneath a thin coating of whitewash. In this way a spacious, ultra-modern though discreet and prudent living room gives way to a cheerful dining room, in which pieces of unusually colored furniture contrast with the diaphanous presence of pieces entirely in white.

The industrially-designed kitchen, dominated almost completely by steel, adapts masterfully to the rather cramped dimensions of a narrow passageway. For its part, the bathroom is entirely clad in wood

Large windows offer exceptional views of the wonderful coastal landscape.

This bedroom is concealed behind a movable partition.

except for the shower, with gresite walls and hidden behind a glass partition.

Like a logical labyrinth in which nobody gets lost, this dwelling divides its rooms with daring and courage. The environments thus created are perfectly harmonious, doing full justice to the privileged exterior.

Its freshness, simplicity and the use of color give this apartment a youthful, relaxed feel, particularly suited to occupa-tion in the summertime, when everything takes on a lighter, more relative meaning.

The main task of the interior designer is usually to interpret the spirit and character of a home's future occupants. In the case of a holiday home, an apartment on the coast or a mountain hide-away though, the owners may specifically want the decor to suggest a different mood and alternative habits. This means that a house may change considerably depending on whether it is the main residence or a holi-day home of the same family.

The modern living room contains an abundance of highly up-to-date furniture.

The wall behind the easy chair is decorated with asymmetrically arranged pictures.

In these cases, the decorator should not be concerned so much with the owners' everyday habits as with their aspirations when they escape from the routine of work and city for a few days.

This is precisely what the designer has achieved here. The apartment's clear, fluid, color-packed spaces actively encourage a less conventional, more relaxed attitude.

This philosophy extends to certain interiors being more suited to a specific time of year or even requiring particular weather conditions. There are rooms which have no meaning without an overcast, rainy sky pressing against the curtains, living rooms which are incomplete without an intransigent sun bouncing off lilos and beach towels, and kitchens that lose heart when the thaw starts and their fire goes out.

Steel reigns in the industrially designed kitchen.

the bathroom combines three of the most up-to-date elements: wood, glazed mosaic and glass.

A trio of aces

These three uncommonly elegant interiors are an example of rhythm, harmony and balance. They are original in design and overcome their spatial limitations with imagination and good taste.

One of the most significant environments is the dining room, characterized by its atmosphere of an avant-garde conference hall: an empty space of generous dimensions and prodigious architecture. The parquet floor offsets the deliberate coldness of the room, a coldness potentiated by the large stretch of glass blocks opened in one of the walls, through which the light penetrates, tempered by mysteri-ous transparencies. The table chosen is a rectangular model with a granite top, while the accompanying chairs are light, simple and black. Against the glass-block wall are paintings, an old trunk and two curious chairs.

The second environment is a space belonging to a larger room: a small living room has been created between two doors that open onto the exterior. Although this is basically a zone of passage, it has been endowed with great warmth thanks to the stove with its smoke stack in full view and the two plant fiber easy chairs. Finally, the bedroom is a masterful transition from one room to the other by virtue of the use of parquet and the walls painted the same color as those of the corridor. The bed is a simple model with a round head, beside which stands a stylized metal bedside table.

Serene, well-balanced spaces constitute pleasant interiors whose attractiveness lies above all in their simplicity and visual cleanliness. And among the decorative resources, the striking glass-block wall shines with its own light.

A zone of passage has been transformed into a fine living room

The bedroom is a masterful entry to the rest of the house.

.In the spacious, avant-garde dining room the traditional ceiling beams are still visible.

An Interior full of life

Cheerful, youthful colors, light that floods the room, gentle contrasts and friendly design furniture together constitute an interior that exudes vitality and freshness.

The different environments of this living-dining room are separated by an attractive interplay of panels and false partitions that define different decorative nuclei. As a whole, the room is perceived as a space of great beauty in which the pieces of furniture and accessories are arranged in a logical, balanced way, fostering ease of movement.

The zone devoted to the living-dining room is delimited by a large, pale wood cupboard, a blue structure —which conceals a practical kitchen— and the terrace doors. A rectangular table on metal legs emerges from the cupboard. Around it, six white chairs resemble stylized armless easy chairs. The necessary touch of originality is provided by the enormous pumpkin-like ceiling light made of thin sheets of wood.

The living-room furniture consists of two springy white sofas with a wooden and glass table in the middle. The natural light is tempered by roller blinds on the doors opening onto the exterior.

Outstanding among the many merits of this interior is the brilliant way in which the different environments have been unified, and the kitchen, enclosed inside blue panels that are transformed in turn into an active part of the decor.

Overall view of the living-dining room, in which it is possible to appreciate the separation of environments.

A rectangular table with steel legs emerges from the cupboard.

Living in a warehouse

Beneath a vaulted roof that conceals the light points lies a huge living room. The decor has transformed an initially cold, unwelcoming space into a genuine home.

The large main room is divided into two different environments: a living room and dining room/kitchen. At the far end, between a number of panels and cupboards, a long corridor leads to the garden. The living area is decorated with two large blue sofas on tiny castors. Between them, like a mobile sculpture, there is a chest, also on castors, full of striking silver spheres. Different sized cushions lie on the sofas, and opposite, an old wooden box acts as the television trolley.

The kitchen design is somewhere between industrial and futurist. Steel predominates, and its structures are light and sketchy. Its elements are arranged in rows, leaving room for a central table. The dining room is perfectly adapted to the characteristics of the kitchen.

Warehouses refurbished as homes are difficult to decorate, due to the risk that they might be cold and impersonal. In this case, thanks to the furniture chosen and the correct spatial distribution, a warm and very welcoming interior has been created.

Overall view of the large warehouse.

The living room decor consists of two large sofas and a chest with silver spheres.

White on white

An overwhelming, eternal white envelops this interior, gently caressing environments characterized by updated classicism and timeless elegance.

Against white walls and on floors of the same color are superimposed pieces of snowy aspect whose outlines disappear, melding with the monochrome surroundings. There is an abundance of classical busts of emperors of old on carved marble columns, creating an atmosphere reminiscent of Roman forums and luxurious patrician residences.

The room has a rectangular floor plan with huge windows opening on either side. Standing against one of the walls is an iron fireplace with the chimney in full view, around which a generously dimensioned sofa, a chesterfield-type sofa and a small occasional table are gracefully arranged. A brightly-colored oriental rug is spread out on the floor. The dining room consists of a

The small corner leads to other rooms in the house.

The large side windows link visually with the false ceiling.

small, light round table accompanied by three metal chairs with upholstery.

There is a small corner near the fireplace concealed behind white garden railings and a heavy curtain. The curtain is gathered on one of its sides by a holder made of leaves. Behind the railings stands a classical sofa entirely in white.

The restrained classicism of the room takes the visitor back to previous periods dominated by cold elegance and the absence of color. Nevertheless, this classicism has been interpreted according to modern tastes: it has been updated and all hints of incoherence or anachronism skilfully avoided.

The thick curtains are gathered by a holder made of leaves.

The white room is divided into two well differentiated environments: living room and dining room.

Sobriety and color

The bathroom is discreetly decorated. The light-colored parquet floor unites both rooms.

Bare brick walls give shape to an austere, sober, solemn bedroom containing few elements only and characterized by light contrasts. Color, introduced in small doses, reduces the dramatic visual effect without being overwhelming.

The sturdy wall against which the bed is placed is crowned by a false agglomerate ceiling that features a discreet light point. Warm wooden flooring links the bedroom to an elegant bathroom, with light tones and polished surfaces. The furniture, of high aesthetic quality, is reduced to indispensable elements: the wooden bed with rectangular head and a simple bedside table. The accessories thus acquire almost vital importance, for without them the bedroom would "die" of absolute boredom. The fuchsia-colored bedspread, the set of pillows and the boxes on the table provide a note of bright, youthful color, offsetting the severity of the room.

For its part, the bathroom is an example of moderation. The predominant cream color is highly suitable for a rather dark space. It contains a single washbasin, while the shower is concealed behind a glass partition.

Small touches of color enliven this bedroom and adjacent bathroom. Applied lighting enhances the beauty of these contrasts and the parquet flooring unites the two environments with serene elegance.

The pillows and the fuchsia-colored bedspread offset the dramatic effect of this bedroom.

Adapting to the environment

The main aim of decoration should be, above all, that of adapting to the environment, to real conditions. Thus it is necessary to study the available space, analyze the possibilities of the different rooms and draw up decoration projects capable of making the most of each individual case. This was the process followed for the interiors that illustrate these pages.

One is a modern kitchen, with a mixture of materials arranged beneath the vaulted roof of a former warehouse. The furniture combines wood, steel and glass in the most natural of ways, and straight lines contrast with the curved surface of the ceiling. The main appliances are contained in a cupboard embedded into the wall and the center of the room is occupied by a long table with steel legs. A surprising note in this postmodern environment is the introduction of a number of rustic details, such as the wicker baskets or the bouquets of dried flowers. The dark linoleum flooring becomes parquet in the dining room.

The second interior is a bathroom, characterized by small dimensions and the predominant use of wood. The marble bathtub occupies the best position, beside the window, and the wall mirror visually duplicates the space.

The industrial-style kitchen lies beneath the vaulted roof of a former warehouse.

A number of rustic elements have been introduced into an essentially postmodern environment.

The search for balance

The space available in this dwelling has been logically and sensibly exploited to create orderly, comfortable and very functional environments. Balance therefore characterizes each of the corners of the house, providing a dynamism that, though desirable, is not always easy to achieve.

The first floor is a huge room divided into different environments: a comfortable living room, a dining room for eight and a study or work area. The living-room wall is covered with a wide wooden bookcase in the center of which there is a movable panel on rails. The seating arrangement consists of two large white sofas and a rocking chair in the same color.

The remaining environments in the room are arranged around the impressive metal stairs. On one side is, a small dining

The wide bookcase with its sliding panel is the main element in the living room.

The most striking piece in the study is the transparent table.

room for four, consisting of a round wooden table and design easy chairs with Alcántara upholstery. The main piece in the study just behind the stair is the original transparent table. Finally, the dining room for eight contains a rectangular table with oblique corners and a set of chairs similar to those in the small dining room, except that these are in wood.

A practical wardrobe with acid-treated glass doors.

The stair is the element around which different environments are arranged.

Open to the exterior

This charming living room is totally open to the exterior through a large glazed door that gives onto the garden. The light that floods in from outside enhances colors and textures.

As a whole, the living room featured on these pages is balanced, serene and makes millimetric use of space, overlooking no corners and avoiding dead spots. One of the walls is clad in wood, providing warmth and offsetting the predominant white. Nonetheless, the true protagonist is the large, electric-blue cupboard next to the glass door.

The furniture consists fundamentally of three visually striking pieces: two identical large white sofas opposite each other and a wooden center table with a glass top. The ultramarine cushions placed on the sofas provide a touch of color.

An acid-treated sliding glass door leads into a long corridor marked with discreet recessed lights in the ceiling. The main element here is the large blue cupboard leaning against one of the walls and totally adapted to the architectural characteristics of the corridor.

This interior illustrates the fact that good ideas are invariably well received, although they should always respond to specific needs.

The blue cupboard is the center of interest.

The furniture consists of two sofas placed opposite each other and a center table.

A maritime character

In a luminous setting of considerable architectural quality, a white, transparent decor attests to the proximity of the sea and gives shape to a refreshing maritime-style interior.

The living room featured on these pages is diaphanous and Mediterranean, reflecting a certain vacation-time serenity. The freshness it exudes is possibly fruit of the predominance of white and blue. There are no further color contrasts (except for the ceramic flooring) or slight touches of color to break the monotony. The fireplace stands against one of the walls, its chimney hidden behind a wide built-in partition with hollows on one side that serve as shelves. The seating arrangement consists of a striped sofa accompanied by a second sofa and an easy chair, both in blue.

The bedroom is painted the same colors as the living room. One corner has been given over to a small study or work area, consisting of an old desk, a wall-to-wall bookcase and a comfortable sofa. At the other end of the room stands the huge double bed with a built-in bedhead.

The prodigious architecture of the dwelling and the strong light from the coastal landscape are the true protagonists of these interiors. The chosen furniture combines in a dignified manner with this elegant setting.

.A study area has been created in the bedroom.

The freshness of the living room is fruit of the use of two colors: white and blue.

Daring elegance

Color forms part of this dwelling, enveloping it and giving rise to audacious contrasts, defining warm homely environments and unexpected corners.

The warmth of the orange-stained wood that covers the floor and sculpts pieces of furniture and false partitions contrasts with the coldness of the shining white of the ceiling or the romantic delicacy of a pastel-blue wall. The outstanding element in the living room is the seating: two large, comfortable electric-blue sofas and an easy chair of the same characteristics. In the center stands a glass-topped table and leaning against the blue wall is a piece of made-to-measure furniture with a number of drawers and doors.

The dining room consists of a stylized rectangular table with a glass top and a set of chairs characterized by their waving backs. Between the glass doors leading outside curious modules used as containers have been placed. A grand piano behind one of the sofas acts as an elegant aesthetic counterpoint.

On leaving this room, the visitor encounters a circular structure that conceals another room. The panels that form this structure feature small windows placed in a row. Opposite, open doors allow one to glimpse a far more conventional second living room.

This dwelling might serve as an example to those who want to decorate their home colorfully and cheerfully, those who wish to be elegant and daring at the same time.

This interior offers beautiful contrasts and very attractive solutions.

The bathroom is tiled throughont with glazed mosaic.

Family life

Exceptionally welcoming and homely, the interiors of this home seem to have been designed for family life. They are replete with logical, practical corners that can be put to excellent use.

By climbing stairs arranged around a central axis we come to the second floor of

A small study stands beside the stair.

an enchanting duplex, decorated with large doses of good taste and imagination. The visitor is received first by a small study consisting of a piece of built-in furniture, wood-faced outside and of stainless steel inside. Decorative objects are of great importance here, particularly the two candlesticks and the huge chess pieces. The parquet floor, of the same color as the piece of built-in furniture, features two low steps that mark a further change in level.

In the bedroom, what most catches the eye is the large closet divided into two parts: one in which to hang suits and long garments and the other with numerous drawers and shelves for folded clothes.

The bathroom is surprisingly bright, colorful and youthful. The pale blue of walls and doors predominates, contrasting with

the white of the furniture. The sanitary ware is concealed behind an acid-treated glass door.

We tend to overlook how much space we actually need to store all our belongings away. Yet if we plan ahead for storage space for everything (and own up to the number of shirts, coats, jackets, pairs of trousers we actually want to keep), not only can we keep everything ship-shape, but all the other rooms in the house will benefit from the existence of spaces which are exclusively designed to store things away.

Old houses often contain rooms without a specific function, and these are the ones which end up being most used. They become wardrobes, junk rooms, workshops or darkrooms: modern houses could take a leaf out of their book.

The closet is the most outstanding element in the bedroom.

Around the fireplace

The different elements that provide this pleasant, spacious living room with its character have been arranged around an iron fireplace with its chimney in full view. In the middle, a large wooden cupboard partially conceals the kitchen.

The white walls, the pale wooden furniture and the white and blue tapestries stand out against the black, opaque slate floor. One of the walls contains a huge wood-framed window through which the room is flooded by natural light. This space is delimited by a wooden bookcase against which a comfortable cushion-covered sofa stands. The seating arrangement is completed by two folding upholstered chairs and two simple stools. A coffee table consisting of two thick wooden sheets stands among these pieces on a plant fiber rug.

The separating element consists on the living-room side of shelves that offset the visual impact of the radiator. The kitchen furniture is arranged in rows, leaving space for a kitchenette characterized by wicker chairs with blue cushions.

Three environments in a single space: living room, kitchen and dining room. All decorated in the same cheerful style.

A large cupboard separates the living room from the kitchen.

The living-room elements are arranged around the iron fireplace.

Upstairs downstairs

This house has just as many doors as are absolutely necessary. This does not mean that the rooms are any less independent though, as a result of intelligent planning of the house's layout and structure over two floors.

Since the early decades of this century, fluidity of space has been one of the great paradigms of modern architecture and design. Compared to traditional structures, new technical possibilities saw the introduction of houses which were more open, freer and less sub-divided; and, at the same time, as habits became more liberal, the demand for this type of space grew. Irrespective of their advantages and drawbacks, houses with large open-plan

spaces and communicating, door-free rooms continue to be a synonym of modernity, liberal habits and progressive ideas. This house also features another essential characteristic of the twentieth century: the primacy of light and brightness. In this respect, psychological well-being is just as important a reason as the physical hygiene which calls for well-lit, ventilated houses.

If we were to sum up our impressions of this house in a few well chosen adjectives, the first words to spring to mind would be natural, healthy, light, peaceful. This is a sure sign that one of the great successes of the designer of this interior has been the creation of an atmosphere of well-being, naturalness and modernity.

Another interesting exercise would be to pick out a detail or piece of furniture from the rest. Of course we would come up with a favorite —the metal fireplace by the terrace, the semi-circular sofa, the bed with fitted drawers—, though we might also realize that these pieces were chosen to create a coherent whole, with a practically homogeneous image, rather than to be appreciated individually.

The materials and finishes are picked up in the different rooms: light-colored wood, white-painted walls, floors in different shades of ocher (honey-colored sandstone downstairs and wood on the top floor), white upholstery and blinds, large glazed surfaces both outside and in…

Two views of the kitchen. Once again, wood is the main material chosen for the finishes.

The stair communicates the living room directly with the master bedroom.

Instead of handles, the doors of the fitted cupboard in the bedroom are equipped with small openings in which to place one's fingers.

Welcoming ambiences

This home reflects the warm, welcoming personality of its owners by offering pleasant corners either for private family life or for animated social gatherings. Everything is vital, cheerful and within reach, and the discreet ambiences will adapt elegantly to the changes brought about by the passing of time.

Reddish tones predominate in the living room: on the parquet flooring, on the modern stylized furniture and on the surface of the walls, stuccoed in salmon pink. The large rug that lies diagonally on the floor also combines reds, oranges, yellows and ochers. Two Alcántara upholstered easy chairs contribute to the predominant color combination, while only the large violet sofas and one of the standard lamps dare to break the chromatic balance by introducing a gentle though very visible con-

trast. At the far end, between two walls, long shelves have been installed. And in certain corners the occasional classic piece offsets the predominant modernity.

The cheerful, well-lit kitchen combines wooden furniture and timber-clad walls with white lacquered furniture and yellow painted walls. The furniture is arranged in

This classic piece stands out against very up-to-date surroundings.

rows and the cooking area has been tiled in white. A round breakfast table has been placed in the center.

The simple bedroom, with access to a small lavatory, features a large double bed with a leather upholstered bedhead and elegant white bedclothes.

Reddish tones predominate in the welcoming living room.

Throughout the house, pictures, wall lamps and any other kind of decorative wall elements are conspicuous by their absence. There are in fact pictures in the house, but all are propped up on shelves, side tables or chests of drawers. In this way, the walls stand out as clear, sharp surfaces.

Parquet flooring is laid all over the house except in the kitchen and bathroom areas to give a sense of continuity. The false ceilings are used to conceal recessed lights in many spots, including the living room, where the warm light of the standard lamp combines with the cold light of the halogen spots in the ceiling.

A youthful lilac-colored corridor leads to the bedroom.

In the center sufficient space remains to create a breakfast area.

In a belvedere

The decor of this luminous, privileged dwelling is entirely without barriers and open to the exterior. The elements are harmoniously arranged and shared out in balanced fashion among different environments.

The living room, dining room and kitchen are contained in a single space of large dimensions. One of the walls is totally glazed, acting as a belvedere with views of the fine surrounding landscape. The living-room area contains a comfortable blue sofa (one of its modules is a chaise longue), a central table in the form of an elegant trolley, and a container on castors that acts as an occasional table.

The dining room is opposite the glazed wall and consists of a simple rectangular table with pale upholstered chairs. The furniture of the kitchen, next to the dining room, is arranged in a "U" shape, while the kitchen itself is separated from the adjoining kitchenette by a light partition.

The bedroom, like the living-dining room, has a pale parquet floor. The beauty of this simple, elegant room is based on economy of elements. The bed, with its upholstered head, is the fundamental piece, although the curious blue stair that leads to the mezzanine half floor also catches the eye. A number of pictures are cleverly arranged on the floor.

The dining room is located beside the glazed wall.

Living room, dining room and kitchen are contained in the same space.

The bathrooms, totally clad in glazed blue mosaic, feature acid-treated glass doors. The ledges are also in translucent glass and contain stainless steel wash-basins.

The two main virtues of this home are its correct unification of environments and its openness to the exterior. The bathrooms, with their translucent doors, contribute further color to the overall decor.

This house is very much influenced by its rather more vertical than horizontal layout.

As the floors are limited in terms of space, it was decided to assign each of them a single function.

The ground floor is the daytime space. A single room provides the setting for all the family's joint activities in the course of the day: living-dining room, kitchen, studio…

While this creates a feeling of space, it also necessitates coherence in the choice of materials in each case. Here, the leading role is taken by light-colored wood, which is used for the dining, coffee and occasion-al tables, shelves and kitchen cupboards, with only the white and other pale, calming colors as a counterpoint.

The night-time area (including bedrooms and bathrooms) occupies the upper floor. It comprises open, functional-looking bedrooms with no aspiration to romanticism or theatricality.

A surprising element in the bedroom is the stair leading to the mezzanine floor.

The bathroom is clad totally in glazed blue mosaic.

Two original offices

Only too often, offices or studios tend to be too serious, boring and even conservative. Times have changed, however, sobriety has ceased to be an unquestionable virtue and freedom of expression, good humor and originality have come to form part of this traditional kind of room.

One of the chosen interiors is filled with curious, unusual elements: a rectangular desk equipped with castors; an oval folding table; a long display case; and a metallic bookcase. The fundamental element is a curious ceiling light consisting of an elaborate network of cables and rings.

Another of the offices contains a desk similar to the previous one, although in this case it is accompanied by a printed easy chair, slender shelves and an elegant solid wood ladder that serves as a bookshelf.

The unusual character of an interior is sometimes a question of details.

Occasionally it is enough to choose an original piece of furniture —such as the desk with folding wings in the third office—, or else special attention may be paid to the facing —the impressive fresco that decorates the walls of the classical studio.

All these environments are different, although they all enjoy the same good basic conditions (large dimensions, abundant light, a regular structure and so on). Full advantage has been taken of their qualities while shunning clichés and conventional concepts.

A highly balanced composition. Outstanding here is the ladder used as a bookshelf.

The wall frescoes are the distinguishing feature of this interior.

Youthful freshness

Like a breath of fresh air, this small, welcoming living room is skilfully and freely decorated. The result is excellent, seeming to have been achieved almost effortlessly, as if by chance, something to which all good decors should aspire. Nonetheless, it is by no means easy to achieve natural decors. They are invariably fruit of elaborate interior designs, since chance is not usually a good counsellor.

Most worthy of praise is the correct arrangement of elements in this living room: spaces and volumes are masterfully combined to produce a balanced environment in which harmony is the keynote. The walls, roller blinds and window frames are all white, thanks to which luminosity and a feeling of spaciousness are gained. The upholstered furniture is also white, and for this reason it seems that its outlines merge with

the overall atmosphere. As the coffee table, a container-type model on castors with a glass top has been chosen. On the floor, a sisal rug adds a note of freshness without attracting too much attention. In one corner stands a small bookcase full of books, records, flowers and personal memorabilia. Finally, the notes of color, though few, have been applied with precision. Thanks to them, this interior acquires life and character.

The small bookcase is full of books, records and personal memorabilia.

Outstanding in this fresh, youthful living room is the correct arrangement of elements.

Color and fantasy

One of the study walls is entirely clad with paintings and photographs.

Nothing in this interior could be accused of being conventional. The changing colors on the walls, the separations between environments, the architectural resources employed, everything seems to flee from the commonplace in search of new solutions, improvising with audacity and breaking away from anything already established.

In the center of a large living-dining room a curious structure emerges: a built-in stair with uneven steps, asymmetrically cutting across each other. As it rises, the brick stair gives way to a much lighter metal spiral staircase that disappears into the floor above. In the living-dining room the walls are yellow, one of them having been decorated with a surprising checkerboard pattern. In the midst of so much color, the furniture is discreet and does not attract too much attention. One of the walls features a large arch that provides access to another room —a highly person-

al library or reading area. This arch, in turn, frames a rectangular door.

Another significant environment in the house is the work area, a large, furnished space with a desk and several folding canvas chairs. The most striking characteristic of this study is the fact that one of the walls is entirely covered by paintings and photographs of different sizes.

This interior has been decorated eclectically, combining elements from a variety of provenances and in a wide range of colors. The result, nonetheless, is a tasteful combination that pleases the eye.

The walls bear witness to the lives and hobbies of the house owners. All together, these images form one big hieroglyphic.

The central stair is the main focus of interest.

Everything is possible

Sometimes anything goes in decoration, and this interior is a good example of the fact: from the deliberate peeling plaster on the ceiling to the police cordon —used to seal off building sites—, which acts as a provocative garland. Nevertheless, the different elements, however surprising they may be, obey the basic rules of balance, harmony and rhythm.

The space is open, since there are hardly any barriers. The furniture, the cladding and the extraordinary murals that decorate the walls are entrusted with the task of separating different environments. The interior architecture improvises and plays with reality, offering partitions that overlap each other and gilt columns that provide a touch of dynamism. Garnet-colored rhomboids have been painted on the bare concrete ceiling. A chaise longue with a gilt back and a classic easy chair together shape the small living area.

The library zone is somewhat classic in its decor: the wooden bookshelf, the rectangular table, the carpet and the leather easy chairs are those that would normally be found in traditional offices. From the ceiling a metallic structure is suspended from which shaded lamps emerge. But as a counterpoint to cliché and conventionalism, a plastic cordon used by the Barcelona City Police has been wound around the metal structure.

The importance of detail and the leitmotif of chance suggest that this living room is designed as a huge three-dimensional collage rather than as an architectural space. The objects and walls seem to have been taken from a variety of contexts, like a Dadaist composition, showing just how the designer has left his mark on this space.

A number of curious decorative elements break the classicism of the library.

An open space in which cladding, colors and murals mark off different environments.

An informal meeting

The corners in this elegant living room are balanced, agile and practical. Movement is easy between the different pieces and everywhere a touch of informality has been maintained.

Few pieces of furniture and generous dimensions are the keys to the success of this decor, in conjunction with the light that penetrates through large glass doors. Attention is concentrated above all on the living area, together with a number of side nuclei that catch the eye and endow the whole with a certain dynamism. The design of the living area is very balanced: three yellow armchairs arranged in the form of a cross and, in the middle, a low light-colored wooden table on a white rug.

Two easy chairs —avant-garde versions of traditional pieces— stand in one corner each, one of them accompanied by a stan-dard lamp and a classical bust. The other corner, possibly more functional, is structured as a leisure area suitable for reading or listening to music. The accompanying elements here are a picture on the wall, the same kind of standard lamp as the one in the other corner, an indoor plant and a series of hanging modules containing a hi-fi set.

Balanced and discreet, the elements in this room have been arranged with skill and precision. The environments thus created are influenced by a gently urbane and highly attractive aesthetic.

Some pieces of furniture, like the coffee table or the shelving modules that house the hi-fi, could have taken their inspiration from the sculptural work of American artist Donald Judd.

A restfully welcoming corner.

The correct arrangement of elements guarantees ease of movement.

Daring elegance

Color forms part of this dwelling, enveloping it and giving rise to audacious contrasts, defining warm homely environments and unexpected corners. The warmth of the orange-Stained wood that covers the floor and sculpts pieces of furniture and false partitions contrasts with the coldness of the shining white of the ceiling or with the romantic delicacy of a pastel-blue wall. The outstanding element in the living room is the seating: two large, comfortable electric-blue sofas and an easy chair of the same characteristics. In the center stands a glass-topped table and leaning against the blue wall a piece of made-to-measure furniture with a number of drawers and doors. The dining room consists of a stylized rectangular table with a glass top and a set of chairs characterized by their waving backs. Between the glass doors leading outside curious modules used as containers have been placed. A grand piano behind one of the sofas acts as an elegant aesthetic counterpoint.

A grand piano acts as an elegant aesthetic counterpoint.

This interior offers beautiful contrasts and very attractive solutions.

On leaving this room, the visitor encounters a circular structure that conceals another room. The panels that form this structure feature small windows placed in a row. Opposite, open doors allow one to glimpse a far more conventional second living room.

This dwelling might serve as an example to those who want to decorate their home colorfully and cheerfully, those who wish to be elegant and daring at the same time.

This circular structure conceals another room. Small windows are placed in a line on its panels.

Between the glass doors curious modules have been placed that serve as containers.

Similar though different

Two similar though radically different toilets, one integrated into the bedroom while the other preserves its privacy. Despite their differences, however, they both share points in common and the same decorative style.

Having a spacious toilet-dressing room right beside the bed is both practical and convenient. Even so, this might cause problems difficult to solve. Toilets are visually cold, while bedrooms are welcoming, relaxing and constitute the best manifestation of their owners' personality. In order to unite both environments, it is necessary to tone down the visual hardness of the toilet and endow the bedroom with a tolerant character. Thus, in one of these interiors the bedroom and toilet meld into each other, giving rise to a new functional and perfectly unified room. The white walls become glazed gray mosaic when they enter the toilet area.

The second toilet is also clad in mosaic, although in this case the color chosen is swimming-pool blue. This room features an interesting interplay of mirrors and both the faucets and the sloping top catch the eye here. Toilets, like other spaces in the home, adapt to the needs and tastes of their users. These two examples are based on the same decorative style, though each one responds to different criteria: the first, for those who opt for functionality and innovation; the second, for those who above all else wish to preserve their privacy.

A series of highly personal touches give the bedroom an informal air. This is the case of the cylindrical box which takes the place of the traditional bedside table, or the lamp that hangs from the ceiling –the model Brera by Italian designer Achille Castiglioni– to replace the usual table lamp.

An eye-catching element here is the slop-ing top.

The toilet gently melds with the bedroom.

A perfect layout

This kitchen shares space with a small dining room, although partial partitions and false walls clearly separate both environments. An impeccable arrangement of elements has made it possible to make the best of corners and the most of the generous spaciousness of this interior.

A long corridor, totally clad in wood and marked with a succession of ox-eyes, leads to the kitchen. This room might pass by completely unnoticed since it is camouflaged behind sliding doors identical to the corridor facing. Having crossed the threshold, the visitor discovers very rational use of space and a pleasant color combination. Gentle coordinates, such as the glazed cream mosaic of the work area and the white of walls and ceiling, are offset by sudden contrasts introduced by the electric - blue furniture and the garnet partition.

The elements in the kitchen zone as such are aligned against the walls, while the cooking and washing-up areas stand opposite each other, thus allowing the user greater freedom of movement. The wall features a very modern set of metallic shelves. The dining area, against the garnet partition, consists of an acid treated glass-topped table with metal legs and four wooden chairs.

By integrating the kitchen and dining room, the former gains elegance and the latter familiarity. Nonetheless, it is still essential to separate environments and differentiate between functions.

The garnet partition and the blue furniture stand out against an otherwise harmonious whole.

The different elements are backed against the wall. The cooking and washing-up areas stand opposite each other.

A long wood-faced corridor leads to the kitchen.

Recovering the past

This spectacular art nouveau apartment, with high ceilings and generous dimensions, had suffered from the harmful effects of the passing of time. Nevertheless, thanks to sensitive refurbishment, it has recovered its past splendor while adapting perfectly to today's needs and tastes. It was necessary to preserve the old structures and fully potentiate the century-old attractiveness of the dwelling. The ceilings were left high and its molding and embossing restored. The flooring has totally recovered its kaleidoscopic design, and the walls, in pale yellow, have acquired a new, gentler character.

In order to furnish a space of such outstanding architectural quality a few very well chosen pieces were used. In the living room, between the two doors of white carpentry, stands a bookcase -type element with glass shelves. The seating arrangement consists of a black leather sofa, a couch like a dentist's chair and an easy chair with red, gray-edged upholstery. Outstanding in the center is an original coffee table with four enormous castors sustaining a fine sheet of glass.

Restoration work, as in this case, must be above all respectful of the past. This apartment is replete with beautiful elements well worth preserving.

It takes very little to transform some spaces, like the hallway shown on the opposite page, into very pleasant places. The original floor tiles and window frames alone, of a quality which is hard to find these days, form a most interesting ambience, which is pointed up by the ceramic jar and seat.

This room enjoys the splendor of a delicately decorated ceiling and the marvelous design of the hydraulic floor.

The corridor is one of the great allies of constructions of the period.

Beneath the waves

The well-chosen dining-room furniture is concentrated near the kitchen.

L ike rolling waves, the roof of this house is divided into a succession of bare brick vaults. The environments beneath follow with distinction the magnificent structures of the house and enhance its beauty.

From the exterior a long corridor leads into the spacious dining room with little furniture, separated from the kitchen by sliding doors. Wood covers practically everything, floors and walls, and provides warmth. The furniture, concentrated near the kitchen, consists of a long pale wood sideboard —next to which a huge vessel has been placed—, a glass-topped table on castors, and four light wicker chairs. A splendid vegetable fiber rug covers the floor. The kitchen is in pale wood, and a counter is visible through its open door.

The spacious dining room is full of empty spaces.

The bedroom is welcoming, well balanced and defined by slow, though constant, rhythms. The center of interest is the large bed with an upholstered head, around which are arranged two bedside tables suspended from the wall, a wicker easy chair, two decorative trunks (one on top of the other) and a stylized bookcase.

Harmony dominates these interiors, a haven of all-pervading peace. The several colours are similar to each other, thus avoiding brusque contrasts and creating an especially relaxing decor.

The angle-poise lamps in the bedroom are a surprising detail which we are more used to finding in an office or on a work desk. They are in fact very practical for reading in bed, as they allow the reader greater mobility and choice of position.

A long corridor leads to the dining room.

The main feature of the harmonious bedroom is the bed with its upholstered head.

The greenish-blue furniture features wooden tops and is arranged along both the walls and a practical central column.

Both kitchens are spacious and their logical layout facilitates ease of movement. Outstanding elements are the ceil-ing skylights.

These are excellent spaces not just for cooking and other household tasks, but also to be enjoyed as alternative living rooms, just as family life in the past used to revolve around the kitchen and the fireplace. As houses became more automated, this room became a clinical room for machines. These two examples express a desire to bring social life back into the kitchen.

The dining room can be seen in the background.

Depth is the outstanding feature of this kitchen, fostered by the correct arrangement of furniture.

Waking up to a patio

The term functionalism often conceals a dictatorship of unacceptable minimums. The speculators of architecture have predetermined what rooms a house should have: living room, dining room, kitchen, bathroom and bedrooms (plus two or three optional spaces: office, dressing room, utility room, junk room, pantry…). The value of the house will depend on the size of these rooms and the number of bedrooms.

Many of domestic architecture's most attractive spaces have been struck out when experts failed to find a pragmatic use for them. Anyone who has a room with a name that has fallen into disuse –a tea room, gallery, observatory, cellar– or with no name at all is sitting on a treasure.

In this house we find one such priceless privilege: a patio next to the bedroom.

Being able to watch the rays of sun creep through the shutters on a Sunday morning as you lie in bed; follow the shadows of the blinds as they move across the walls; linger over the newspaper with a cappuccino and croissant as you sit in the patio; warm yourself in this winter sun trap. All absolutely dispensable activities, but who would not rather dispense with other things to be able to enjoy them?

There are a few give-away signs that the original building is an old one: the masonry wall at the head of the bed, the hand-crafted door frames, the high ceilings.

The designers have made every effort to extend this aesthetic to the rest of the house. The materials used in other rooms such as the recently renovated kitchen and bathroom, plus the furnishings and fittings chosen, echo images of days gone by. The photograph of the bathroom shows us a washbasin fitted in marble with a single gold-colored tap, and the floor tiles are used on the walls, too. In the kitchen, the cupboards have louvered doors and the marble kitchen sink presents a strong contrast with the vitroceramic cooker top; nostalgia meets high-tech.

View of the bathroom. The colors range through natural and earthy tones.

In the kitchen. The row of tall furniture conceals the extractor hood.

The house's bedrooms are set out around a patio. Views from the facing windows superpose different scenes.

Visual continuity

The long wooden wall of the living-dining room, transformed into a bookshelf and superim posed on the pillars and party wall of the dwelling, is prolonged until it links with the corridor, although to delimit different environments it is interrupted by a blue false partition. Thanks to this practical resource, the interiors exude an elegance and naturalness that enchant the visitor.

The screen-bookshelf does not reach the ceiling; the room therefore breathes from above and the sensation of being excessively enclosed is avoided. The dining area features a sofa upholstered with striped electric-blue cloth. The coffee table is a model consisting of a single wood and stainless steel leg topped by a sheet of glass.

The dining room is outstandingly simple and discreet, decorated with a rectangular walnut-finished table and walnut chairs with Alcántara upholstery.

The kitchen, for its part, is a white room with furniture aligned in rows. From one of the ceramic-clad walls emerges a table with a metal leg.

This home features perfectly balanced interiors in which each piece is in its right place. Nevertheless, rather than being forced, rigid or imposed, this balance appears to be absolutely natural, the result of informality and everyday living.

The long partition-bookshelf links the dining room and corridor.

Each piece seems to occupy its rightful place.

Orange filter

This living room, with its warm, orange-colored light, has collected together objects from various sources and the most diverse of styles. The designer has applied two parallel strategies: the use of color to give the room unity and a miscellany of details to fill corners.

The stoneware floor tiles echo traditional clay adobes. The walls are painted with a sponge to break the homogeneous surface up into waters. The same system has been applied to the ceilings.

The room is elongated with a skylight in the centre and French windows at the end, revealing a small back garden with a tree, enclosed by a wall.

The various sectors of the room are arranged as a series of planes: study, library, dining room, living room and garden. This ensures that the various activities contained in this one room are clearly differentiated.

Almost all the furniture is marked by the same sensibility, discernible in its classic lines, a profusion of molding and dark-toned woods. And the latent customs of its occupants are hinted at in the glass doors of the cupboard where the chinaware is kept, the roll-top of the writing desk, the embroidered white tablecloth and the vase of lilies.

Changing levels

An interminable bare brick
wall visually dominates
this interior decor.

The spaces of this majestic, restful dwelling are determined by the different ceiling levels that rise and fall giving shape to narrow, elegant rooms, unexpected and marvelous.

From the main salon (whose decor is based on a certain restrained rigor), in which the gaze is drawn upwards, subsequently to be lost in the furrows of an interminable bare brick wall, the visitor may freely enter (there are no rigid barriers) a far more secluded room with a vaulted ceiling. The changes in level succeed each other smoothly, as if unintentional. They are there, nevertheless, originally and astonishingly beautiful.

Seen from above, the layout of the main salon is perfectly balanced, its central elements arranged in the form of a cross. An original wavy-lined sofa stands against the bare brick wall, accompanied by a second sofa of more conventional lines, two red easy chairs (the note of colour is never lacking) and an iron fireplace with the draft in full view. In the center, an elegant table with a fine glass top.

An original decorative
complex beneath
the bare brick vault.

142

The space covered by the vaulted ceiling has been left practically empty, except for the decorative elements around an unusual iron and glass table and a panel acting as a separating element.

Balance, visual clarity and the combination of volumes are the reigning qualities of this house, whose success lies in the fact that each space has been assigned the importance it deserves.

A traditional structure like the vaulted ceiling is combined with modern concepts such as open-plan space and up-to-the-minute details to produce an ambience that is open to interpretation.

The layout of this salon is perfectly balanced, its elements arranged in the form of a cross.

The space delimited by the vaulted ceiling has been left practically empty.

Unusual structures

The structures of a house delimit and give shape to its environments. The available space, the format of each room and the more or less inconvenient corners of a house all depend on the structures. As an example, we have chosen an interior in which columns, sloping ceilings and partitions create complicated settings.

At one end of the room there is a huge central partition that acts as the visual link between two floors while at the same time separating environments and providing privacy. This structure is painted in a cream similar to that of the false ceiling, both of which contrast with the reddish tone of the parquet. Behind the partition is a living room, of which the photograph shows only a yellow easy chair and a series of modules hanging from the wall.

The living room extends into a long corridor interrupted by two partial transversal partitions with a bookcase in be-tween. At the end, fitting perfectly between two walls and a sloping ceiling, stands a large, functional writing desk. Both pieces of furniture are made of the same wood that clads one of the walls.

In this dwelling, structures occupy the visual foreground, since they are too strikingly original to pass by unnoticed. The furniture discreetly performs its decorative function, harmoniously and delicately integrated into its surroundings.

The furniture selected here could be likened to sculptures: opposite, one of the aristocratic chairs by Ch. R. Mackintosh in the foreground, and an avant-garde model by Dutchman Gerrit Rietveld.

*The large partition
links two floors.*

*Partial false partitions
interrupt the corridor.*

Contained passion

A sloping ridge roof and an intense red are the factors conditioning the appearance of this multi-purpose space: living room, studio, library… The center of the room is occupied by a stairway leading upwards. Its handrail consists of a glass upright with chrome-plated supports and a tubular banister in the same material. The use of these materials prevents this element from interrupting visual communication with the center the room.

One end is laid out as a study area, the other for relaxation, with a bright-blue corner sofa in lively contrast to the reddish tones used for the wall. The upholstery on the sofa is edged in red, and the cushions heaped casually on it are the same color as the wall, this time trimmed in blue to create a play on the alternation of color. The sofa is surrounded by paintings of very different periods, styles and sizes. In the center the decorators have placed a predominantly blue and red carpet, on which stands a glass-centered table on castors.

The wall against which the sofa is set is just high enough for people to sit comfort-

Views of the living room under the ridge roof. The decorators have based their choice of colors on the contrast between bright red and blue.

Detail of one of the corners to either side of the stairway. The standard lamps, the telescope in the studio and the ventilator on the little table create a grouping of vertical elements dotted strategically around the room.

ably, and the decorators were even obliged to build a wooden-topped brick, shelf there to separate the sofa slightly from the wall. It is the sharply sloping roof which produces this situation, creating dual effect: firstly, a feeling of protection and tranquillity (which psychologists could justify from many points of view), and secondly preventing its dominating the room, although it is one of it most frequented spots. Elements such as the clock, the weathervane and the boxing gloves serve as a counterpoint to the books. The background of the bookshelf picks up the blue theme.

The living room is covered with parquet flooring. The ground is at different levels, to differentiate the various uses contained in this space.

Detail of the dining room area. The standard lamp bathes the entire space in a warm yellow light. Although the color scheme is different from the living room upstairs, certain elements, such as the blue armchair and the maroon curtains, pick up the colors used there.

Empty space

In this curious interior there is scarcely any furniture or decorative objects, since they are unnecessary. The space is so impressive and the architectural resources so innovative that items of furniture would act merely as visual obstacles.

The empty, bare living room is overwhelmingly vast. Reminiscent of a gymnasium, its floor is completely covered with parquet. The walls have been left white except for horizontal red lines that enhance the perspective. The ceiling, also in white, is interrupted by long, narrow skylights that admit natural light.

At the far end, behind a sheltering glass partition, two floors can be seen linked by a light stair characterized by its slight curve, transparent steps and wooden handrails. The entry is on the floor below, and the only pieces of furniture visible are a couple of modern-design metallic chairs.

The floor above receives the visitor with a long, oval, glass-topped central table. Each of the two sides of the room features a semicircular glazed space containing counters, one of which contains a sink and long faucets.

The beauty of this already impressive interior is enhanced by the lighting arrangement.

This great room doubles up as living room and squash court, with the space above turned into a perfect gallery from which to follow the game. These mixed spaces combine radically different functions which make them particularly suggestive.

Gently curving stairs link the two floors.

Overall view of the room.

In an art nouveau palace

This splendid art nouveau home, with the city at its feet, is inspired by the mosaic fragments of the Park Güell and the undulating forms of the architecture of Gaudí.

The interior environments coexist in friendly harmony with and without concealing the prestigious constructional forms, drawing from them and enhancing their beauty. Kaleidoscopically designed mosaics partially cover the walls, sharing the space with colored wallpaper and vivid paintings, in combination with elaborate moldings and original friezes, Moorish arches and rosettes that crown tall, imposing windows. It is precisely in the area enclosed by a set of these windows, and beneath a spectacular vaulted ceiling, that a sober, distinguished dining room has been created, featuring avant-garde furniture. In another of the house's luminous rooms a study has been installed, decorated with very up-to-date furniture and elements characteristic of modern life.

Mosaics, wallpaper, paintings and friezes decorate the walls of this interior.

The dining room lies beneath a vaulted ceiling in a space of sumptuous architecture.

Its decor is an example of absolute sobriety and deliberate restraint. Totally clad in marble, its furniture is reduced to a slab of the same material —into which the steel washbasin is sunk—, a mirror and a display stand for sweets, here used to keep different objects in.

The architecture of this home is of elaborate, exuberant beauty. The furniture and accessories discreetly cede the leading role to the setting that accommodates them.

This would not have been possible with an imitative or kitsch decor; conversely, by emphasizing the modernity of the furnishings, the architectural setting is highlighted.

The bathroom is the only place in the house that does not share the exuberant baroque style of the rest.

Modern furniture has been chosen for the study in order to update the 19th-century atmosphere.

Serene reality

A serenity beyond times and fashions reigns over this interior of white walls and restrained contrasts, in which furniture and decorative objects are neatly arranged to create pleasant corners and clearly differentiated environments.

This square, well-proportioned living-dining room opens uninhibitedly to the exterior through large glazed sliding doors. Light penetrates even the most unexpected corners, so that interior and exterior meld into a single harmonious image. In the living area large modern elements, such as the two white and blue-striped sofas, visually offset more gracefully classic pieces like the twin easy chairs. A round table in solid wood stands in the center. On the other hand, the dining-room furniture consists of a light, glass-topped table and wood and canvas movie-director type chairs. At the far end, built-in stairs

without handrails lead to the floors above, while a corridor opens onto the terrace.

The white walls contrast with the rustic, hard-wearing reddish sandstone that forms the flooring. Two oriental rugs provide attractive notes of color, while an iron fireplace with the chimney in full view occupies one of the corners.

This peaceful interior is characterized by a steady, meticulously calculated rhythm. Nevertheless, what might otherwise have been a rigid symmetry is broken by elements such as the rugs and the indoor plants.

The resulting calculated disorder encourages a more relaxed, user-friendly enjoyment of the space. A chair can be moved, slippers left lying by the couch or the newspaper spread out on the table with no fear of upsetting a painstaking arrangement.

General view of this serene living-dining room.

The dining room is beside built-in stairs without handrails.

Making the most of corners

In the form of a narrow corridor, the space of this interior has been meticulously arranged, making full use of corners. On the other hand, the center has been left free to facilitate circulation and avoid cramming.

The long, straight room has doors at both ends that open onto the exterior. The original, eye-catching ceiling consists of several brick vaults supported by sturdy concrete beams. The floor is reddish terracotta, which enlivens and reinforces the color combination, while the walls are painted white and pale lilac, the two tones perfectly differentiated. The most outstanding built-in pieces are the stair with wrought iron handrail and the gently curving fireplace.

The stair separates two environments: the living room on one side and the kitchen on the other. The living-room furniture is arranged around the lilac fireplace: a comfortable oriental-print sofa with large cushions, a wicker coffee table, a wooden table with a large lampshade on top, a wooden easy chair and a built-in piece similar to the fireplace.

The kitchen is also the dining room. The cheerful red furniture is arranged in rows in line with an old trunk and an old display-case type cupboard. Opposite, a light table with a wicker top and wrought-iron legs.

This interior is youthful, colorful and delicately naïf. Full use has been made of the space and architectural elements act as separators. Color enlivens and gives character to ensembles of innocent beauty.

The fundamental constructional elements are the built-in stair and the fireplace.

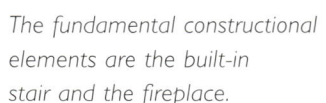

The cheerful red kitchen furniture is arranged in rows.

Living in the city

It is a well-known fact that the main problem of houses in cities is a lack of space. The high cost of urban land forces us city-dwellers to squeeze as much as we can out of every square foot. On these pages we present two bedrooms which overcome their small dimensions to produce an extraordinary overall effect.

The first of them stands on what used to be a terrace. Aluminum and glass were used for the structure, which was then lined with parquet flooring, rendered walls and a false ceiling. The final effect is very similar to any other bedroom in the house, but with far better natural lighting.

The width of the bedroom is taken up completely by the bed, leading the decorators to substitute a conventional bedstead with a continuous parquet platform which forms a step in the floor. Opposite the bed stand a table, a stool and a carpet. A series of cylindrical wooden drawers for storing hats is used to conceal the essential bedroom accoutrements. Clothes and all other accessories are kept in another room. These few elements are suitably arranged to create a comfortable bedroom. There are of course some obvious objections: the lack of space makes it rather difficult to get into bed, and it is always much more convenient to have a wardrobe inside the bedroom; however, these home-owners would not be able to have another bedroom if they were to insist on these conditions.

While the means of getting round the lack of space in the second example are not identical, the two designs do share some very clear characteristics which help

Two complementary views of a single bedroom from either end.

The choice of a tatami as the base for the bed ruled out the use of the traditional bedside table. Here, lamps and bedtime reading are placed directly on the floor.

us to see the advantages of certain decisions. As in the first example, the bed is at very low-level, in this case standing on a tatami (the plant-fiber surface traditionally used to cover floors in Japanese houses), practically at floor level. This is not mere coincidence: a low bed occupies less space and visually creates a broader perception of the room.

Then the decorators decided not to use doors to separate the bedroom from the adjacent living room. While the existing stretch of wall allows a degree of independence between the two spaces, the two openings resolve the problem of lack of space in the bedroom.

This layout gives way to an interesting play of varying settings on different levels, to which the designers have applied an intelligent use of color for greater effect. The living room, painted with cold tones (blue, white and mauve), leads into a bedroom in the background which is full of warm, welcoming light. The opposite effect is created in the bedroom, which exudes comfort and coziness as opposed to the freer, more open space of the living room.

The choice of a tatami as the base for the bed ruled out the use of the traditional bedside table. Here, lamps and bedtime reading are placed directly on the floor.

Opposite page: a view of the bedroom from the living room. The mauve-painted door in the background leads into the bathroom.

Good ideas

ood decorative projects provide ideas that solve problems and satisfy needs. The interiors of this cheerful, casual home are full of practical solutions and intelligent resources.

The elements of the living-dining room are arranged around a large terrace which is also a summer dining room. The sometimes dazzling light from outside is tempered by sturdy white roller shades. The living room, of an elegance somewhere between austerity and romanticism, is situated next to the glass doors that give onto the exterior. The protagonist of the seating arrangement is the large white sofa with two bookcases behind. These book-cases do not reach the ceiling, so enough space was left to create a cornice on which several ceramic pieces stand. In the mid-dle, opposite the sofa, coffee table stands on a sisal rug. From the side of one of the bookcases emerges a flap that acts as a work desk.

On the terrace an enchanting summer dining room has been created.

From the side of one of the bookcases a flap emerges that acts as a work desk.

The dining room stands beside a wooden structure that encloses a room. This structure features three large windows, and on one of its sides there are shelves with urns. An acid-treated glass door that slides on rails conceals this peculiar construction. The dining-room table is a stylized model with a glass top. The iron chairs are grey upholstered.

The decor, apart from embellishing an environment, should also increase the home-owners' comfort. This house offers numerous fine corners that also contain especially practical solutions.

The idea of beauty is completely subjective, and is frequently the result of our sensation of comfort.

The bookcases do not reach the ceiling, leaving room for a cornice with ceramic pieces on top.

The interior of the wooden structure.

In pink and blue

Thanks to their predominant color, these two interiors are spectacular and very out of the ordinary. Pink in one case and sky blue in the other endow complicated, almost empty spaces with originality and life.

Pink enlivens the corridors and areas of passage in this barn-like dwelling, and totally covers what would otherwise be ugly piping, transforming it into a curious decorative element. This piping enters the loft where the gable roof is joined, a space whose interior surfaces have been clad in wood. One of the walls has also been faced with fine timber boards, while the tall glazed door to the exterior is divided into attractive quarters. The gray ceramic floor combines very well with the pale pink of the walls. At the far end it is possible to appreciate built-in stairs that seem to be a prolongation of the floor, although their plaster side has been painted pink with a gray border.

The second interior is a bathroom tiled with sky-blue mosaic. The corner in the photograph contains few, though very well balanced, elements.

Thanks to the color and the use of pale wood, these interiors are transformed into youthful, fresh, cheerful and casual spaces.

The bathroom, clad in blue gresite, has been decorated with only a few pieces of furniture.

Color tempers the harsh presence of the imposing pipes.

Well defined

These two interiors have something in common: the perfection of their firm and well defined lines, their balanced spaces and their harmonious color combinations. All is perfection, equilibrium; there are no discordant notes. They are environments designed to be lived in, full of vitality and far removed from the cold decors of catalogs and decoration manuals.

One of the photographs shows a two-story home in which the partially projecting wooden stair captures almost all the attention. The ground floor, with its terracotta flooring, contains a dining room located opposite large glazed doors and composed of a glass table and its respective chairs; a passage area decorated only with an original dresser and a brightly colored oriental rug; and a bright, cheerful kitchen which opens onto the exterior. The rooms on the floor above are hidden behind a false wooden partition.

For its part, the bathroom is the product of the most revolutionary design trends. Two stainless steel washbasins with piping in full view are half sunk into the marble ledge. The long, elegant faucets match the accessories that adorn the room. A large mirror visually duplicates the space. The wall is clad in glazed white gresite while at the top, almost touching the ceiling, it features a discreet border.

The smaller the space, the more meticulous the design called for. All the elements in this bathroom have been reduced to their minimum expression. The basis of the decoration is quality in its materials and simplicity of form.

The bathroom is the product of avant-garde design trends.

In this home, the stair that links the two floors is the main protagonist.

A vitalist decor

Some interiors are visually relaxing; they are serene spaces that calm the spirit and temper the senses. By contrast, the vitalist decor of this house animates the spirit.

One of the main spaces is the study, covered by a false ceiling of strips of plastic. The walls are clad in ocher Venetian stucco while the flooring is black, shining marble.

At the far end, a crammed book-case stands between the two walls, while the work chair is a classic piece with floral upholstery. Natural light enters through glazed doors that open onto the exterior.

The most cheerful room is the brightly-colored kitchen. The furniture, arranged in a "U" shape, combines wood-colored pieces with others lacquered in yellow. The

The upholstery of the easy chair, the armchair and the original winged table combine to create a youthful environment.

The gentle Venetian stucco enlivens the study and endows it with freshness.

walls are painted yellow, although the work area is covered with tiles in shining bottle-green, the same color that enlivens the floor and an oval table that emerges from the units and rests on a strong steel leg.

In the mosaic-clad bathroom, the bathtub is partially concealed behind a partition. The ceramic washbasin is sunk into a piece of wall-to-wall furniture.

The occasional discreet touch of color, an original piece of furniture here and there, an eye-catching print, any detail, however simple it may be, can enliven an environment and transform it into a unique space.

The bathtub is concealed behind a partial partition.

A table emerges from the units and rests on a steel leg.

Brought up to date

This slightly rustic home has been decorated with noble, valuable, and perfectly restored pieces. Nevertheless, the environments thus obtained are neither classic nor traditional. Historical furniture, possibly part of a family legacy, is combined with modern, youthful elements, giving rise to rooms of great freshness and beauty.

The living and dining rooms, in which most of the social life of the house takes place, stand on a rectangular terrazzo floor. The living room, the ceiling of which features a number of recessed lights, is full of vitality and elegantly though casually furnished. The seating arrangement consists of two check-upholstery sofas around a simple glass-topped table. At the far end

there is a second living room containing two sturdy easy chairs upholstered in electric blue and a wooden coffee table. The most outstanding piece, however, is the antique filing cabinet.

Outstanding elements in this living room are the two sturdy easy chairs and the antique filing cabinet.

General view of the two living areas.

In the master bedroom, painted in the same colors as the living-dining room, the furniture is arranged like in a hotel suite; that is, there is a bedroom as such and a small living area.

The kitchen is cheerfully colorful and luminous. Small country-style closets live harmoniously side-by-side with modern furniture.

When decorating a house with antique furniture it is not necessary to restrict oneself to classic ambiences. In this case, the period pieces are integrated into youthful, fresh interiors.

The kitchen is surprisingly colorful.

The bedroom is arranged like a hotel suite.

The house of the future

Incredible structures from this original, innovative and daring home. Its interiors are as striking as the exterior and the furniture and decor accessories disappear in the midst of peculiar, complicated forms.

Columns, pillars, cornices and large glazed walls have taken possession of the house, creating dramatically empty, powerful spaces of irregular outline. One of the facades endows the building with the appearance of a glass box, since the interior can be seen through it, a white interior in which only a picture and a curious easy chair dare to break the solitude.

The walls are white and the floor is paved in marble of the same color. One room is presided over by the strikingly personal bottle green of the psychedelic easy chair.

The totally glazed facade.

The curious easy chair stands out as the only piece of furniture.

The bedroom furniture consists merely of a large double bed and a couple of simple bedside tables, one of which features a small orange lamp. The most striking element in this room is the beam structure that decorates the ceiling.

Houses such as this one that are characterized by their revolutionary architecture must be decorated with care, since any form of excess, however small or insignificant it may be, could upset the aesthetic balance.

The beam structure is the most striking element in the bedroom.

Inside, numerous interplays of light and shade are created.

The heart of the house

This is a room that exudes vitality, in which long hours will surely be spent reading, conversing and devoted to social and family life. It is a comfortable space in which nothing is superfluous or in the way: everything responds to specific needs.

Next to the stair leading to the floors above, the big, rectangular living room is dominated by pale wood (the parquet floor, the stair and its handrails, the door leading to the kitchen). At one end of the room a pleasant dining area has been created consisting of a square extendible table and a set of plant fiber chairs. A stylized sideboard stands against the wall. In a corner next to the stair stand a bar and a drinks trolley.

Presiding over the other end of the room is a large, built-in, wall-to-wall bookcase featuring an open fireplace with the chimney concealed. Arranged around the bookcase is an exceptionally welcoming and homely living area. The seating arrangement consists of a comfortable white sofa, an easy chair in the same color and a rocking chair. In the center, three small tables are arranged in a right angle.

Once the main pieces of furniture have been chosen, attention must be paid to the accessories, to the decor, to all those details that make a home one's own. In this case we would make special mention of the lamps, the paintings and the cushions.

The dining room, with its extendible table and plant fiber chairs, lies beneath the stair.

The three small tables arranged in a right angle are a distinguishing element of the living room.

The plant kingdom

The most significant aspect of these two interiors is the use of plant fiber, which covers walls and floors as well as forming part of some of the furniture. Its adds its own particular touch of freshness to elegant, luminous environments, transforming them into unique spaces characterized by their casual, youthful personality.

The living room is regular and well-proportioned, totally surrounded by large glazed doors divided into quarters. The vaulted false ceiling consists of numerous stylized canes, while the floor is covered by an interminable carpet of plant fiber. The green-framed windows filter the strong sunlight through yellow curtains. The seating arrangement consists of two large cream upholstered sofas with a wide strip of striped textile, and two wicker chairs. The center of the room has been left practically empty except for a number of coffee tables. Behind one of the sofas is a simple dining room consisting of a rectangular folding table and three garden chairs.

The bedroom also lies beneath a vaulted ceiling, and its doors giving onto the terrace, the curtains and the floor are identical to those of the living room. The large, elegant double bed features a rounded head and romantic bed linen. At its side stands a classic solid wood bedside table.

Unity is something fundamental in a home. However different the rooms may be, they should reveal the same spirit and maintain an overall personality.

Behind one of the sofas a simple dining area has been created.

The bedroom follows the same decorative patterns as the living room.

The vaulted ceiling, the carpet and the two youthful chairs are all in plant fiber.

A fairy tale

Colors, lights and curious shapes are given free rein in this original interior, to create an ensemble of magical beauty in which everything seems possible. The furniture acquires new meaning, while conventional furniture is seen from a new, daring perspective.

The discreet pale yellow walls soften the visual impact of a highly varied and variegated ensemble, thus preventing the visitor's gaze from becoming lost among so many colors. But this is where the discretion ends: all the rest is exuberance and daring. The large, comfortable sofa stands out thanks to its audacious upholstery, characterized by large blue and yellow squares that cover the seat, backrest and armrests. The personality of this piece contrasts with a wavy-lined easy chair in surprising red upholstery. In the center, the movable glass-topped design table on castors is both attractive and very practical.

The dining room is in a corner, between two columns. The round table rests on a single leg attached to the floor. Around it are arranged four timber-frame chairs, each with differently colored upholstery. One end of the room features a circular structure clad in glass blocks.

The visitor's first impression on contemplating this interior is of a cheerful space full of vitality, suggesting that the owners of the house are young, carefree, fun-loving people who like to experiment and want nothing to do with conventionality.

The yellow walls discreetly soften the visual impact of the wide variety of colors.

The dining room stands between two columns. Outstanding elements here are the chairs with their different colored upholstery.

A summer dining area

During the summer months, life in the open air becomes an imperious necessity. For this reason, gardens, sometimes neglected in the course of severe winters, are recovered, galleries refurbished and balconies and patios exploited to the full. Such is the case of the terrace featured here.

The terrace crowns an urban block in the center of a bustling city. Since it was formerly impossible to relax in this part of the house, a remedy had to be found, and this took the from of a latticework partition placed all around to gain privacy: from sober brick plant pots, vines climb mischievously up the lattices.

In order to create an effect of welcoming familiarity, on the floor two warm-colored oriental rugs have been spread out that perfectly match the terra-cotta tiling. The seating arrangement consists of an elegant garden bench and an easy chair in the same style; the center table is a circular-topped model with sturdy turned legs; cheerful decorative elements are arranged on the floor: two white cushions, a bowl of fruit, a metal watering can, etc.

The decoration of a terrace must follow the same rules as that of interiors. The objective is to achieve a welcoming environment that is full of life, and all resources are valid to attain this end.

A trellis provides the terrace with privacy and isolates it from the outside world.

A fine, balanced composition: wooden furniture and interesting objects.

Country style brought up to date

The traditional rustic style takes us back to days gone by when we lived in close contact with nature, and when the house -the home- was unchanging in the face of passing years, a guardian and protector of customs, values and memories. But times change, and we live in a period of transformations and trials. This rustic, welcoming house therefore breaks with tradition and adapts its country style to present-day tastes.

As a general rule, the kitchen is the living heart of country houses: they are warm and welcoming spaces, designed for family life, and the kitchen illustrated here is no exception. Its thick walls and vaulted ceilings enclose a colorful room, full of vitality. The furniture is ranged along one of the walls, leaving the center free for a dining table.

The stair landing, an explosion of color, is another space which is worthy of particular mention, with its yellow and orange walls, green-framed windows and white and striped sofa covers.

The kitchen windows reveal just how thick the walls are.

The landing presents a gorgeous color contrast.

A peaceful refuge

lthough combined with whites, with natural wood and the clay tones of the floor tiles and mosaic, it is blue which reigns supreme in every corner of this bedroom and its adjoining bathroom: walls, ceiling, furnishings, bed linen and upholstery. It really is fascinating to see how the extensive use of a single color affects our perception of a space, quite independently of questions of taste and sensibility; here we find a particularly intense and lovely color: the color of the skies of the Matisse cut-outs, of Jujol's ceilings and, in its most concentrated version, of the monochrome Yves Klein canvases. Firstly, it is used to establish associations between normally very unrelated, disparate elements which would otherwise be impossible; then a dialogue is created, a play on similarities and contrasts which is somehow much more in keeping with the plastic arts than a spatial vision of things.

Detail of the wash basin. The dark wood unit blends in perfectly with the rest of the bathroom furnishings, like the terra-cotta floor or the mosaic friezes.

Touches of color

The pieces of furniture that decorate these interiors are cheerful, original and entertaining. Their design is picturesque, far removed from monotony and boredom, and their daring forms conceal intelligent resources, conceived to solve problems of space. To all this we must add enchant-ing touches of color: striking, differentiating brush strokes that reveal not a hint of conventionalism.

One of the rooms we feature here is a youthful, carefree dining area. The central part is presided over by a large colored piece of furniture that acts as a dividing panel, behind which a small study is hidden. This piece consists of different wooden parts and containers of considerable dimensions, rising above a harlequinade base that joins up with the high skirting board. The table chosen is remarkably original: it consists of colored legs (some brown and the others yellow) on which two superimposed glass sheets rest. The chairs are also a tour-de-force of originality, with their undulating backrests and seats.

Another room selected here is the enchanting bathroom. One of its most striking elements is the applegreen walls. The washbasin is an avantgarde stainless steel model with the plumbing in view, while the walls have been decorated with small, naif children's drawings.

A large, curiously designed piece of furniture separates the dining room from a small studio.

The most surprising element in the bathroom is its apple-green walls.

Zone of passage

Two wings of the same dwelling are joined by a long corridor that links both parts with such elegance that it acquires value in its own right, its own personality, a unique, differentiating character often unknown to zones of passage. The success of this arrangement lies in the fact that care has been lavished on even the tiniest detail, and this corridor has been considered as a fundamental part of the house.

Consecutive transparent glass sheets give shape to a reality that is part magical, part summery, the main attraction of which is its visual simplicity. The corridor is lit by discreet recessed lights in the ceiling. A glass wall separates the corridor from the rest of the interior, acting as a soft architectural barrier.

The interior features pale wood parquet flooring that potentiates the natural light that enters through numerous glass doors. The dwelling is characterized by roomy, open interiors. Next to the glass wall of the corridor an unusual wooden bench offsets the predominant emptiness.

The materials —glass, wood, sandstone— used to build and shape this dwelling are all entirely modern, creating elegant environments that demand the scantiest of decors.

Discreet recessed lights illuminate the corridor. The facade consists of modern sandstone walls.

An unnsual bench stands beside the glass partitions.

Experimental decoration

Decoration, like art, must be prepared to innovate, to incorporate new, unusual pieces -in short, to experiment with available resources to modify and re-interpret reality. In this particular case, apparently incompatible elements have been combined and fantastic, revolutionary structures created.

The key space in this ultra-modern home is a large room split into two essential environments: living room and kitchen. The different decors are arranged beneath a false slatted ceiling linked to another, more conventional ceiling (that corresponds to the kitchen area), white like the walls with their recessed lights. The transi-tion from living area to kitchen area is marked by a huge wooden bookcase containing a large number of disks. In the center of this arched structure is a writing desk with a portable computer.

The living-room furniture is arranged asymmetrically around two windows protected by roller blinds. Between them, a rectangular mirror seems to have been placed to deliberately upset the balance. In the center of the room a large metal sink unit informs visitors that they are in the kitchen, while an unusual candle-holder on the floor provides a touch of avant-garde eccentricity.

The living room in the background, and the kitchen in the foreground, are at once joined and separated.

The separating structure features a collection of disks and a practical writing desk.

The coldly —almost icily— elegant bathroom is pure design. It is totally enveloped in translucent blue glass, while in the ceiling a few discreet recessed lights provide tempered, relaxing light. At the far end, a vertical sheet of glass conceals the toilet behind. The wooden bath is surprisingly warm in such a cold setting. The loft above reveals the house's final surprise: a magnificent roof observatory.

A modern observatory has been created in the gable roof.

The bathroom is totally enveloped in blue translucent glass.